"Cacao trees with pods of purple and gold,
hold secrets of chocolate, a story to be told."

Once upon a time, in a bustling city filled with tall buildings and busy streets, lived two young children named Tom and Ellie. Tom was a clever and curious boy, while Ellie was sweet and kind-hearted, finding joy in the simplest of things. Both shared a common passion for adventure.

One sunny day, as Tom and Ellie were exploring a nearby park, they stumbled upon a hidden pathway. It sparkled with a mysterious glow, as if inviting them to discover something extraordinary. Their eyes met, and with a shared sense of wonder, they stepped on to the unknown path.

As they ventured further, their surroundings completely changed. The cityscape faded away, replaced by a vibrant, magical chocolate forest. This forest had no ordinary trees; instead, it was filled with chocolate ones, with bright leaves and dark, tall trunks, engulfing the place in a bittersweet aroma.

Wandering in this enchanted chocolate forest, Tom and Ellie marveled at the delectable sights. The air was filled with the aroma of chocolate, making their mouths water. They quickly plucked some of the chocolate leaves. While they were busy nibbling on the chocolate, they were suddenly distracted by a gentle voice. A bright young talking cacao bean greeted them with a cheerful smile and a twinkle in his eye.

"Hello, little explorers! I am Coco, in charge of this lovely chocolate forest. Beware! follow me closely or you're bound to get lost." Sensing the children's excitement and eagerness to learn more, Coco decided to share the incredible story of chocolate - making with them. He led them towards one end of the chocolate forest, where they could witness each step of this magical process.

Coco said, "this small gated farmland at the brink of the forest is for growing cacao. In it stand tall cacao trees ladened with colorful fruits called cacao pods." He explained, how these pods were like treasure chests, as, they contained the precious cacao beans from which chocolate is made. Tom and Ellie dreamily looked at the different colors and shapes of the pods, ranging from vibrant yellows to deep purple.

Coco then took them to a group of farmers who were
carefully cutting the ripe cacao pods from the trees.

Coco even encouraged Tom and Ellie to try their hand on plucking the ripe pods from the trees.

Next, Coco led them to a shed where he demonstrated how to extract the cacao beans from the pods. He took a small knife, slit open a pod, and revealed a cluster of beans covered in a soft, sweet pulp. He offered some to the children, who enjoyed the tangy, refreshing flavor.

Coco continued, "These beans need to undergo fermentation to develop their characteristic flavors." He showed Tom and Ellie how the beans were placed in large, shallow containers covered with banana leaves, where microorganisms worked their magic in transforming the beans.
The strong, unpleasant aroma during fermentation made the children wrinkle their noses.

Coco then turned to the children and smiled.

After fermentation, Coco led them to a drying area where the beans were spread out to dry naturally, under the warm sun, Tom and Ellie watched as the slimy, purple-tinged beans transformed over days into dry, brownish-colored ones. Coco emphasized the importance of proper drying to achieve the best chocolate flavor.

Coco then turned to the children and said, "Now it's time for some roasting to get that deep, intense chocolatey flavor that you love."

He demonstrated how the roasted beans were crushed using a heavy stone grinder, slowly turning them into a thick, fragrant paste known as chocolate liquor. The children took turns grinding and feeling the beans transform under their hands.

Coco explained, the chocolate liquor needed further refining and smoothening. He took them to a special machine called a conche, which mixed and heated the chocolate liquor for hours. The conching process enhanced the smoothness and texture of the chocolate, making it melt in the mouth.

Coco collected the liquor and said, "Now it's time to turn it into a lovely slab of chocolate. Let's add the rest." He poured in milk powder, sugar, and a touch of vanilla, explaining how these ingredients enhanced the flavor and sweetness. They watched as the mixture blended together, creating a luscious, chocolatey concoction.

Coco explained, that this concoction had to be cooled and poured into molds for hardening. He took the children to an air-conditioned room, which had to be kept between 20°C and 25°C. Here, he poured the chocolate mixture into molds of various shapes and sizes. Tom and Ellie patiently watched as the liquid chocolate solidified.

Finally, Coco took them to a charming packaging station, where the finished chocolate treats were lovingly wrapped and adorned with colorful labels. Tom and Ellie couldn't help but imagine the joy on people's faces as they received these delectable creations.

Having witnessed the entire chocolate-making process, from cacao pod to packaged chocolate, Tom and Ellie felt a deep appreciation for chocolate makers.

They thanked Coco for sharing the secret of chocolate-making with them.

They bid farewell to Coco and stepped back onto the hidden pathway, determined to share their newfound knowledge about chocolate with everyone they knew.

1. Tom and Ellie found a magical path leading to a vibrant

_____________ forest.

2. The talking cacao bean that guided them was named

_____________.

3. Cocoa butter is known for its smooth and _____________

properties.

4. The process of developing the flavors of cacao beans is called

_____________.

5. Cacao is rich in _____________ and iron, making it very

beneficial for health.

6. _____________ and Ellie are the two young adventurers in the

story.

Let's find answers...

Rakesh Saini - Chocolatier, educator and cacao consultant. Always playful with cacao beans.

Shveta K - Baker, food enthusiast and writer at heart.

Know more about us - https://chocolatesbyrakeshsaini.com/